CW01160084

A Hug For Harriet

By
Glenn S. Guiles
Illustrated by
Raymond J. Whalen

For as long as Harriet could remember, things had been a certain way. Each day the same things happen. Every day was the same.

Each morning as the sun began to shine, she and the other miniature donkeys would let the farmer know they were hungry. They would call out, "*Hee haw, hee haw! It's time for breakfast! It's time for our oats and hay!*"

After breakfast, Harriet would spend the day walking around her pasture playing and exploring with the other donkeys. When evening came, the herd again called out until the farmer brought the donkeys more to eat.

When the food was gone, the donkeys quieted down for another night's sleep.

Harriet noticed that she was the smallest of all the donkeys. No new donkeys had arrived in the time she had lived there either. She decided that she must be the youngest!

Harriet's coat was entirely white except for small circles of black hair under each of her large, dark eyes. She also had other black markings of various sizes on her sides. She had a short mane of white hair and a short, scraggly tail. A tail comes in very handy when a donkey needs to keep the flies away!

There were many donkeys in the herd. Twelve or more! Harriet only knew two of them well. One was a gray and white female named Sally. The other was an almost completely gray male named Nacho.

Harriet is very impressed with Sally because she had two names! Sally had a habit of pushing the other donkeys out of her way by kicking up her back legs and wildly waving her head up and down. One day, Harriet heard the farmer say, "Sally, since you are always so full of energy and always causing a commotion, I am going to call you Spitfire Sally!"

Harriet's other friend, Nacho, was much calmer and quieter. He was quite a bit bigger than Harriet. He was bigger than Sally too! He was much more polite to the other donkeys and spent most of his time just watching the day's events from a distance. Harriet enjoyed having two friends who are so different!

Harriet was never been able to get very close to the farmer who brought the food. Each day when mealtime arrived, all the bigger and older donkeys rushed to the food. They all pushed ahead of her. By the time Harriet got close to the hay and oats, the farmer was gone.

Not getting close to the farmer made Harriet sad. She saw the farmer scratching the other donkeys' ears and patting their sides. To Harriet this looked wonderful!

As Harriet was thinking about how nice it would be to get some attention from the farmer, she saw something she had never seen before. A red pickup truck with a trailer backed up to the pasture gate. The farmer put halters on Sally and Nacho's heads and led them to the trailer.

This made Harriet worry. She thought, "*Where are my friends going without me?*" All of a sudden, Harriet found a halter being placed on her head. She was taken to the trailer right along with Sally and Nacho. Harriet felt better. She was excited to be going on an adventure with her friends!

The three donkeys filed into the trailer one by one. The back doors closed and the truck pulling the trailer began to move. The truck's engine grew louder and softer as it pulled the trailer up and down hills. The trailer bounced up and down. It bounced from side to side. *"This is very different from any other day I can remember!"* thought Harriet.

The truck and trailer stopped moving. The back doors of the trailer slowly opened with a loud scr-e-e-ech. Harriet looked out in surprise. She, Sally and Nacho were no longer at the farm where they had always lived! This place was different!

All three donkeys were led off of the trailer and guided to a large pasture with a fence all around. Harriet could see that the pasture had many trees on one side. On the other side was a small barn. It would be a dry place to get out of the wind and rain. Next to the gate she could see a large tub of water. "A thirsty donkey can get a nice drink of water there," she thought.

After the truck and trailer had left, a man that Harriet had never seen before came over to the pasture gate. He was carrying a bucket of oats and a large bunch of hay. Harriet was so excited. "With only two other donkeys, I can get right up close!" she thought.

Harriet could see the man's face. He had friendly eyes and a great big smile. He said, "Hello, Sally! Hello, Nacho! Hello, Harriet! I am your new owner. My name is Mr. Michael."

Harriet could not get over what an incredible day this had been! She had moved to a new home with her friends and she had met a person right up close. And then the best thing happened to Harriet...

Mr. Michael put his arms around Sally's neck and hugged her. Then he hugged Nacho's neck and then Harriet's neck. He also scratched their ears and patted their sides. This is what I've always hoped for! Harriet loved her new home.

Harriet thought, "I have lots of oats and hay to munch on and lots of water to drink. I have my two friends to keep me company. My new owner scratches my ears and gives me pats and hugs. My new home is the best place in the world. I am so happy!" Harriet couldn't wait to see what other wonderful things would happen on Mr. Michael's farm.

But Harriet decided that, even though all of these new things were great, the hug from Mr. Michael was definitely the best!

More books about Harriet the Miniature Donkey
by
Glenn S. Guiles

Harriet's BIG
Adventure

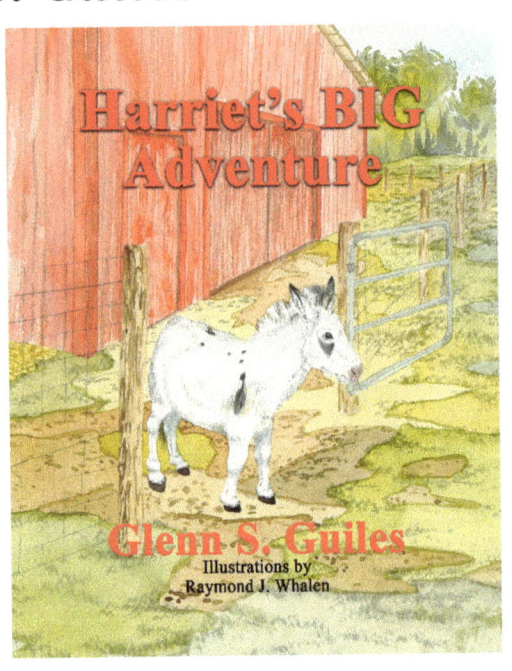

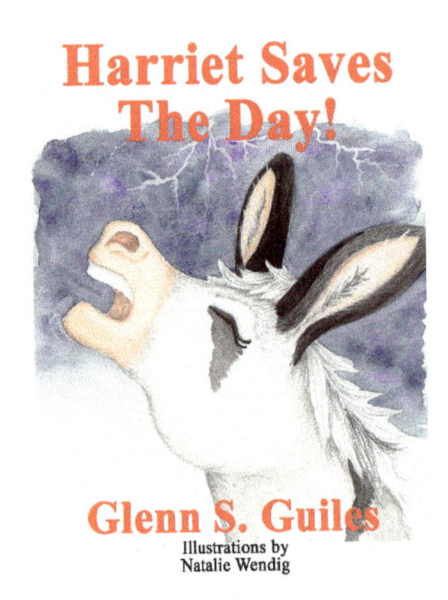

Harriet Saves
the Day!

Both available on Amazon and Barnes & Noble

Milton Keynes UK
Ingram Content Group UK Ltd.
UKHW050959201123
432902UK00003B/24